100 FAVORITE PRAYERS AND BIBLE VERSES

Christine A. Dallman

Publications International, Ltd.

Christine A. Dallman is a freelance writer who has contributed to the devotional publication *The Quiet Hour* and is a former editor and columnist for *Sunday Digest* magazine. She is the author of *Daily Devotions for Seniors,* an inspirational resource for maturing adults, as well as coauthor of *How to Let God Help You Through Hard Times* and *If Jesus Loves Me, How Do I Know?*

ACKNOWLEDGMENTS:

All Scripture quotations are taken from the *New Revised Standard Version* (NRSV) of the Bible. Copyright © 1989, by the Division of Christian Education of the National Council of the Churches of Christ in the USA.
Used by permission. All rights reserved.

COVER CREDIT: Planet Art Collection

Copyright © 2008 Publications International, Ltd. All rights reserved. This book may not be reproduced or quoted in whole or in part by any means whatsoever without written permission from:

Louis Weber, CEO
Publications International, Ltd.
7373 North Cicero Avenue
Lincolnwood, Illinois 60712

Permission is never granted for commercial purposes.

ISBN-13: 978-1-4127-1394-8
ISBN-10: 1-4127-1394-3

Manufactured in China.

8 7 6 5 4 3 2 1

A JOURNEY OF REDISCOVERY

The pages of this book contain samplings from a great sea of communication between God and humankind. As you read through the selections, you may find that the passages are familiar in two ways: one, you will have read or memorized a prayer or Scripture in the past; or two, you will be able to identify with what the author of the prayer or passage is writing about because you've "been there."

These favorites are sure to evoke the kind of fondness that only an old friend can stir in our hearts. And yet, as you take time to read them in a new context, you may find them fresh as the day you discovered them.

During the process of rediscovery, you may wonder why these passages and prayers remain favorites from age to age. What is it about them that causes so many of us to single them out and hold on to them? The quality of timelessness stems from the combination of truth and universal human experience.

People often say a phrase "rings true" when it has that certain something that can withstand the tests of time and scrutiny. We hope this is what you will find as you peruse the pages of *100 Favorite Prayers and Bible Verses.* May you, in these familiar words, find the blessing of timeless truth that renews itself each time we open our hearts to it.

To help you find your favorite prayers and Bible verses, several appendices at the end of this book list the pages of famous prayers and Bible verses in this book, as well as Scripture passages whose themes relate to love, peace, and faith. So rediscover and enjoy old favorites, or find new prayers and Bible verses to inspire and sustain you.

THE LORD'S PRAYER

Our Father in heaven,
hallowed be your name.
Your kingdom come.
Your will be done,
on earth as it is in heaven.
Give us this day our daily bread.
And forgive us our debts,
as we also have forgiven our debtors.
And do not bring us to the time of trial,
but rescue us from the evil one.

MATTHEW 6:9–13

Hear, O Israel: The Lord is our God, the Lord alone. You shall love the Lord your God with all your heart, and with all your soul, and with all your might.

DEUTERONOMY 6:4–5

Naked I came from my mother's womb, and naked shall I return there; the Lord gave, and the Lord has taken away; blessed be the name of the Lord.

JOB 1:21

For everything there is a season, and a time for every matter under heaven: a time to be born, and a time to die; a time to plant, and a time to pluck up what is planted; a time to kill, and a time to heal; a time to break down, and a time to build up; a time to weep, and a time to laugh; a time to mourn, and a time to dance; a time to throw away stones, and a time to gather stones together; a time to embrace, and a time to refrain from embracing; a time to seek, and a time to lose; a time to keep, and a time to throw away; a time to tear, and a time to sew; a time to keep silence, and a time to speak; a time to love, and a time to hate; a time for war, and a time for peace.

ECCLESIASTES 3:1–8

For God so loved the world that he gave his only Son, so that everyone who believes in him may not perish but may have eternal life. Indeed, God did not send the Son into the world to condemn the world, but in order that the world might be saved through him.

JOHN 3:16–17

INSTRUMENT OF PEACE

*L*ord, make me an instrument of thy peace.
Where there is hatred, let me sow love;
Where there is injury, pardon;
Where there is doubt, faith;
Where there is despair, hope;
Where there is darkness, light;
Where there is sadness, joy.
O divine master, grant that I may not
so much seek to be consoled as to console,
to be understood as to understand,
to be loved as to love;
For it is in giving that we receive,
It is in pardoning that we are pardoned,
It is in dying that we are born
to eternal life.

FRANCIS OF ASSISI

*F*inally, beloved, whatever is true, whatever is honorable, whatever is just, whatever is pure, whatever is pleasing, whatever is commendable, if there is any excellence and if there is anything worthy of praise, think about these things.

PHILIPPIANS 4:8

Be strong and courageous; do not be frightened or dismayed, for the Lord your God is with you wherever you go.

JOSHUA 1:9

*B*ut do not ignore this one fact, beloved, that with the Lord one day is like a thousand years, and a thousand years are like one day. The Lord is not slow about his promise, as some think of slowness, but is patient with you, not wanting any to perish, but all to come to repentance. But the day of the Lord will come like a thief, and then the heavens will pass away with a loud noise, and the elements will be dissolved with fire, and the earth and everything that is done on it will be disclosed. . . . But, in accordance with his promise, we wait for new heavens and a new earth, where righteousness is at home. Therefore, beloved, while you are waiting for these things, strive to be found by him at peace, without spot or blemish.

2 PETER 3:8–10, 13–14

A GOLDEN-RULE PRAYER

*I*ncline us O God! to think humbly of ourselves, to be saved only in the examination of our own conduct, to consider our fellow-creatures with kindness, and to judge of all they say and do with the charity which we would desire from them ourselves.

JANE AUSTEN

Who will separate us from the love of Christ? Will hardship, or distress, or persecution, or famine, or nakedness, or peril, or sword? As it is written,

"For your sake we are being killed all day long; we are accounted as sheep to be slaughtered."

No, in all these things we are more than conquerors through him who loved us. For I am convinced that neither death, nor life, nor angels, nor rulers, nor things present, nor things to come, nor powers, nor height, nor depth, nor anything else in all creation, will be able to separate us from the love of God in Christ Jesus our Lord.

Romans 8:35–39

The heavens are telling the glory of God;

and the firmament proclaims his handiwork.

Day to day pours forth speech,

and night to night declares knowledge.

There is no speech, nor are there words;

their voice is not heard;

yet their voice goes out through all the earth.

and their words to the end of the world.

Let the words of my mouth and the meditation

    of my heart

be acceptable to you,

O Lord, my rock and my redeemer.

PSALM 19:1–4, 14

*J*esus said to them, "I am the bread of life. Whoever comes to me will never be hungry, and whoever believes in me will never be thirsty."

JOHN 6:35

*T*herefore, since we are surrounded by so great a cloud of witnesses, let us also lay aside every weight and the sin that clings so closely, and let us run with perseverance the race that is set before us, looking to Jesus the pioneer and perfecter of our faith, who for the sake of the joy that was set before him endured the cross, disregarding its shame, and has taken his seat at the right hand of the throne of God.

HEBREWS 12:1–2

*T*he fruit of the Spirit is love, joy, peace, patience, kindness, generosity, faithfulness, gentleness, and self-control. There is no law against such things. And those who belong to Christ Jesus have crucified the flesh with its passions and desires. If we live by the Spirit, let us also be guided by the Spirit.

GALATIANS 5:22–25

*L*ove your enemies, do good to those who hate you, bless those who curse you, pray for those who abuse you.

LUKE 6:27

PRAYER FOR SUCCESSFUL ENDEAVORS

*O*Lord, let your ear be attentive to the prayer of your servant, and to the prayer of your servants who delight in revering your name. Give success to your servant today, and grant him mercy!

NEHEMIAH 1:11

But this I call to mind, and therefore I have hope: The steadfast love of the Lord never ceases, his mercies never come to an end; they are new every morning; great is your faithfulness. "The Lord is my portion," says my soul, "therefore I will hope in him." The Lord is good to those who wait for him, to the soul that seeks him.

LAMENTATIONS 3:21–25

ANSWERS

My prayers, my God, flow from what I
　　am not;
I think thy answers make me what I am.
Like weary waves thought follows upon thought,
But the still depth beneath is all thine own,
And there thou mov'st in paths to us unknown.
Out of strange strife thy peace is strangely wrought;
If the lion in us pray—thou answerest the lamb.

GEORGE MACDONALD

18

*A*ll scripture is inspired by God and is useful for teaching, for reproof, for correction, and for training in righteousness, so that everyone who belongs to God may be proficient, equipped for every good work.

2 TIMOTHY 3:16–17

What then are we to say about these things? If God is for us, who is against us? He who did not withhold his own Son, but gave him up for all of us, will he not with him also give us everything else?

ROMANS 8:31–32

$\mathcal{P}$eace I leave with you; my peace I give to you. I do not give to you as the world gives. Do not let your hearts be troubled, and do not let them be afraid.

JOHN 14:27

$\mathcal{T}$he end of the matter; all has been heard. Fear God, and keep his commandments; for that is the whole duty of everyone. For God will bring every deed into judgment, including every secret thing, whether good or evil.

ECCLESIASTES 12:13–14

FOR A NATION AT WAR

*W*ith malice toward none, with charity to all, with firmness in the right as God gives us to see the right, let us strive to finish the work we are in, to bind up the nation's wounds, to care for him who shall have borne the battle and for his widow and his orphan, to do all which may achieve and cherish a just and lasting peace among ourselves and with all nations.

ABRAHAM LINCOLN

For to me, living is Christ and dying is gain.

PHILIPPIANS 1:21

GOD IS ABLE

*A*h Lord God! It is you who made the heavens and the earth by your great power and by your outstretched arm! Nothing is too hard for you.

JEREMIAH 32:17

*H*e has told you, O mortal, what is good; and what does the Lord require of you but to do justice, and to love kindness, and to walk humbly with your God?

MICAH 6:8

I lift up my eyes to the hills—
from where will my help come?
My help comes from the Lord,
who made heaven and earth.
He will not let your foot be moved;
he who keeps you will not slumber.
He who keeps Israel
will neither slumber nor sleep.
The Lord is your keeper;
the Lord is your shade at your right hand.
The sun shall not strike you by day,
nor the moon by night.
The Lord will keep you from all evil;
he will keep your life.
The Lord will keep
your going out and your coming in
from this time on and forevermore.

PSALM 121

For by grace you have been saved through faith, and this is not your own doing; it is the gift of God—not the result of works, so that no one may boast. For we are what he has made us, created in Christ Jesus for good works, which God prepared beforehand to be our way of life.

EPHESIANS 2:8–10

$\mathcal{B}$e kind to one another, tenderhearted, forgiving one another, as God in Christ has forgiven you.

EPHESIANS 4:32

$\mathcal{S}$ee what love the Father has given us, that we should be called children of God; and that is what we are. The reason the world does not know us is that it did not know him. Beloved, we are God's children now; what we will be has not yet been revealed. What we do know is this: when he is revealed, we will be like him, for we will see him as he is. And all who have this hope in him purify themselves, just as he is pure.

1 JOHN 3:1–3

*B*ut be doers of the word, and not merely hearers who deceive themselves. For if any are hearers of the word and not doers, they are like those who look at themselves in a mirror; for they look at themselves and, on going away, immediately forget what they were like. But those who look into the perfect law, the law of liberty, and persevere, being not hearers who forget but doers who act—they will be blessed in their doing.

JAMES 1:22–25

*T*herefore I tell you, do not worry about your life, what you will eat or what you will drink, or about your body, what you will wear. Is not life more than food, and the body more than clothing? Look at the birds of the air; they neither sow nor reap nor gather into barns, and yet your heavenly Father feeds them. Are you not of more value than they? And can any of you by worrying add a single hour to your span of life? And why do you worry about clothing? Consider the lilies of the field, how they grow; they neither toil nor spin, yet I tell you, even Solomon in all his glory was not clothed like one of these. But if God so clothes the grass of the field, which is alive today and tomorrow is thrown into the oven, will he not much more clothe you?

MATTHEW 6:25–30

MARY'S SONG

*M*y soul magnifies the Lord,
And my spirit rejoices in God my Savior,
for he has looked with favor on the lowliness of
    his servant.
Surely, from now on all generations will call me
    blessed;
for the Mighty One has done great things for me,
and holy is his name.
His mercy is for those who fear him
from generation to generation.
He has shown strength with his arm;
he has scattered the proud in the thoughts of
    their hearts.
He has brought down the powerful from their
    thrones,
and lifted up the lowly;
he has filled the hungry with good things,
and sent the rich away empty.

He has helped his servant Israel,

in remembrance of his mercy,

according to the promise he made to our
    ancestors,

to Abraham and to his descendants forever.

LUKE 1:46–55

Have you not known? Have you not heard? The Lord is the everlasting God, the Creator of the ends of the earth. He does not faint or grow weary; his understanding is unsearchable. He gives power to the faint, and strengthens the powerless. Even youths will faint and be weary, and the young will fall exhausted; but those who wait for the Lord shall renew their strength, they shall mount up with wings like eagles, they shall run and not be weary, they shall walk and not faint.

ISAIAH 40:28–31

*T*hough the fig tree does not blossom, and no fruit is on the vines; though the produce of the olive fails, and the fields yield no food; though the flock is cut off from the fold, and there is no herd in the stalls, yet I will rejoice in the Lord; I will exult in the God of my salvation. God, the Lord, is my strength; he makes my feet like the feet of a deer, and makes me tread upon the heights.

HABAKKUK 3:17–19

$\mathcal{D}$o not let your hearts be troubled. Believe in God, believe also in me. In my Father's house there are many dwelling places. If it were not so, would I have told you that I go to prepare a place for you? And if I go and prepare a place for you, I will come again and will take you to myself, so that where I am, there you may be also.

JOHN 14:1–3

$\mathcal{F}$or I have no pleasure in the death of anyone, says the Lord God. Turn, then, and live.

EZEKIEL 18:33

$\mathcal{S}$eek the Lord while he may be found, call
upon him while he is near; let the wicked forsake
their way, and the unrighteous their thoughts; let
them return to the Lord, that he may have mercy
on them, and to our God, for he will abundantly
pardon. For my thoughts are not your thoughts,
nor are your ways my ways, says the Lord. For as
the heavens are higher than the earth, so are my
ways higher than your ways and my thoughts than
your thoughts. For as the rain and the snow come
down from heaven, and do not return there until
they have watered the earth, making it bring forth
and sprout, giving seed to the sower and bread to
the eater, so shall my word be that goes out from
my mouth; it shall not return to me empty, but it
shall accomplish that which I purpose, and suc-
ceed in the thing for which I sent it. For you shall
go out in joy, and be led back in peace; the mountains and the hills before you shall burst into
song, and all the trees of the field shall clap their
hands. Instead of the thorn shall come up the

cypress; instead of the brier shall come up the myrtle; and it shall be to the Lord for a memorial, for an everlasting sign that shall not be cut off.

ISAIAH 55:6–13

Since, then, we have a great high priest who has passed through the heavens, Jesus, the Son of God, let us hold fast to our confession. For we do not have a high priest who is unable to sympathize with our weaknesses, but we have one who in every respect has been tested as we are, yet without sin. Let us therefore approach the throne of grace with boldness, so that we may receive mercy and find grace to help in time of need.

HEBREWS 4:14–16

The spirit of the Lord God is upon me, because the Lord has anointed me; he has sent me to bring good news to the oppressed, to bind up the brokenhearted, to proclaim liberty to the captives, and release to the prisoners; to proclaim the year of the Lord's favor, and the day of vengeance of our God; to comfort all who mourn; to provide for those who mourn in Zion—to give them a garland instead of ashes, the oil of gladness instead of mourning, the mantle of praise instead of a faint spirit. They will be called oaks of righteousness, the planting of the Lord, to display his glory.

ISAIAH 61:1–3

RELIANCE

O Lord, never suffer us to think that we
Can stand by ourselves, and not need thee.

JOHN DONNE

*Now faith is the assurance of things hoped
for, the conviction of things not seen.*

HEBREWS 11:1

*F*inally, be strong in the Lord and in the strength of his power. Put on the whole armor of God, so that you may be able to stand against the wiles of the devil. For our struggle is not against enemies of blood and flesh, but against the rulers, against the authorities, against the cosmic powers of this present darkness, against the spiritual forces of evil in the heavenly places. Therefore take up the whole armor of God, so that you may be able to withstand on that evil day, and having done everything, to stand firm. Stand therefore, and fasten the belt of truth around your waist, and put on the breastplate of righteousness. As shoes for your feet put on whatever will make you ready to proclaim the gospel of peace. With all of these, take the shield of faith, with which you will be able to quench all the flaming arrows of the evil one. Take the helmet of salvation, and the sword of the Spirit, which is the word of God. Pray in the Spirit at all times in every prayer and supplication. To that end keep alert and always persevere in supplication for all the saints.

Ephesians 6:10–18

*W*e know that all things work together for good for those who love God, who are called according to his purpose.

ROMANS 8:28

*T*his is my commandment, that you love one another as I have loved you. No one has greater love than this, to lay down one's life for one's friends. You are my friends if you do what I command you.

JOHN 15:12–14

*T*rust in the Lord with all your heart,
and do not rely on your own insight.
In all your ways acknowledge him,
and he will make straight your paths.

PROVERBS 3:5–6

*If any of you is lacking in wisdom,
ask God, who gives to all generously and
ungrudgingly, and it will be given you.*

JAMES 1:5

PRAYER OF CONFESSION AND REPENTANCE

*H*ave mercy on me, O God,
according to your steadfast love;
according to your abundant mercy
blot out my transgressions.
Wash me thoroughly from my iniquity
and cleanse me from my sin....
Purge me with hyssop, and I shall be clean;
wash me, and I shall be whiter than snow....
Create in me a clean heart, O God,
and put a new and right spirit within me.
Do not cast me away from your presence,
and do not take your holy spirit from me.
Restore to me the joy of your salvation,
and sustain in me a willing spirit.

PSALM 51:1–2, 7, 10–12

I pray that, according to the riches of his glory, he may grant that you may be strengthened in your inner being with power through his Spirit, and that Christ may dwell in your hearts through faith, as you are being rooted and grounded in love. I pray that you may have the power to comprehend, with all the saints, what is the breadth and length and height and depth, and to know the love of Christ that surpasses knowledge, so that you may be filled with all the fullness of God.

Now to him who by the power at work within us is able to accomplish abundantly far more than all we can ask or imagine, to him be glory in the church and in Christ Jesus to all generations, forever and ever. Amen.

EPHESIANS 3:16–21

BOOKMARK OF
TERESA OF AVILA

*L*et nothing disturb you
nothing frighten you,
all things are passing;
Patient endurance
attains all things:
one whom God possesses
wants nothing
for God alone suffices.

TERESA OF AVILA

O Lord, our Sovereign,
how majestic is your name in all the earth!
You have set your glory above the heavens.
Out of the mouths of babes and infants
you have founded a bulwark because of
      your foes,
to silence the enemy and the avenger.
When I look at your heavens, the work of
      your fingers,
the moon and the stars that you have
      established;
what are human beings that you are mindful
      of them,
mortals that you care for them?
Yet you have made them a little lower than God,
and crowned them with glory and honor.
You have given them dominion over the works
      of your hands;
you have put all things under their feet,
all sheep and oxen,
and also the beasts of the field,

the birds of the air, and the fish of the sea, whatever passes along the paths of the seas. O Lord, our Sovereign, how majestic is your name in all the earth!

PSALM 8

And Jesus came and said to them, "All authority in heaven and on earth has been given to me. Go therefore and make disciples of all nations, baptizing them in the name of the Father and of the Son and of the Holy Spirit, and teaching them to obey everything that I have commanded you. And remember, I am with you always, to the end of the age."

MATTHEW 28:18–20

PRAYER BEFORE WORK

My God, you are always close to me.
In obedience to you, I must now apply
myself to outward things. Yet, as I do so,
I pray that you will give me the grace of
your presence. And to this end I ask that
you will assist my work, receive its fruits as
an offering to you, and all the while direct
all my affections to you.

BROTHER LAWRENCE

The Lord bless you and keep you;
the Lord make his face to shine upon you,
and be gracious to you;
the Lord lift up his countenance upon you,
and give you peace.

NUMBERS 6:24–26

So if you have been raised with Christ,
seek the things that are above, where Christ
is, seated at the right hand of God. Set
your minds on things that are above, not on
things that are on earth, for you have died,
and your life is hidden with Christ in God.

COLOSSIANS 3:1–3

$\mathcal{B}$lessed are the poor in spirit, for theirs is the
kingdom of heaven.

Blessed are those who mourn, for they will
be comforted.

Blessed are the meek, for they will inherit the earth.

Blessed are those who hunger and thirst for
righteousness, for they will be filled.

Blessed are the merciful, for they will receive mercy.

Blessed are the pure in heart, for they will see God.

Blessed are the peacemakers, for they will be called
children of God.

Blessed are those who are persecuted for
righteousness' sake, for theirs is the kingdom
of heaven.

Blessed are you when people revile you and
persecute you and utter all kinds of evil
against you falsely on my account. Rejoice and
be glad, for your reward is great in heaven.

MATTHEW 5:3–12

In the beginning was the Word, and the Word was with God, and the Word was God. He was in the beginning with God. All things came into being through him, and without him not one thing came into being. What has come into being in him was life, and the life was the light of all people. The light shines in the darkness, and the darkness did not overcome it.

JOHN 1:1–5

PRAYER FOR BOLDNESS

Sovereign Lord, who made the heaven and the earth, the sea, and everything in them, . . . grant to your servants to speak your word with all boldness, while you stretch out your hand to heal, and signs and wonders are performed through the name of your holy servant Jesus.

ACTS 4:24, 29–30

For all who are led by the Spirit of God are children of God. For you did not receive a spirit of slavery to fall back into fear, but you have received a spirit of adoption. When we cry, "Abba! Father!" it is that very Spirit bearing witness with our spirit that we are children of God.

ROMANS 8:14–16

*H*e was despised and rejected by others; a
man of suffering and acquainted with infirmity;
and as one from whom others hide their faces he
was despised, and we held him of no account.

Surely he has borne our infirmities and carried
our diseases; yet we accounted him stricken,
struck down by God, and afflicted. But he was
wounded for our transgressions, crushed for our
iniquities; upon him was the punishment that
made us whole, and by his bruises we are healed.

Isaiah 53:3–5

"Everyone who calls on the name of the Lord shall be saved." But how are they to call on one in whom they have not believed? And how are they to believe in one of whom they have never heard? And how are they to hear without someone to proclaim him? And how are they to proclaim him unless they are sent? As it is written, "How beautiful are the feet of those who bring good news!" But not all have obeyed the good news; for Isaiah says, "Lord, who has believed our message?" So faith comes from what is heard, and what is heard comes through the word of Christ.

ROMANS 10:13–17

A CONSTANT PRAYER

*L*ord, if this be Your will, so let it be.
Lord, if this is good and profitable, give me
grace to use it to Your glory. But if it be
hurtful and injurious to my soul's health, then
remove this desire from my mind, I pray.

THOMAS Á KEMPIS

*W*ithout faith it is impossible to please
God, for whoever would approach him must
believe that he exists and that he rewards
those who seek him.

HEBREWS 11:6

I give you a new commandment, that you love one another. Just as I have loved you, you also should love one another. By this everyone will know that you are my disciples, if you have love for one another.

JOHN 13:34–35

This book of the law shall not depart out of your mouth; you shall meditate on it day and night, so that you may be careful to act in accordance with all that is written in it. For then you shall make your way prosperous, and then you shall be successful.

JOSHUA 1:8

At that time the disciples came to Jesus and asked, "Who is the greatest in the kingdom of heaven?" He called a child, whom he put among them, and said, "Truly I tell you, unless you change and become like children, you will never enter the kingdom of heaven. Whoever becomes humble like this child is the greatest in the kingdom of heaven. Whoever welcomes one such child in my name welcomes me.... Take care that you do not despise one of these little ones; for, I tell you, in heaven their angels continually see the face of my Father in heaven."

MATTHEW 18:1–5, 10

PRAISE FOR WISDOM
AND REVELATION

*B*lessed be the name of God from age to age,

for wisdom and power are his.

He changes times and seasons,

deposes kings and sets up kings;

he gives wisdom to the wise

and knowledge to those who have understanding.

He reveals deep and hidden things;

he knows what is in the darkness,

and light dwells with him.

To you, O God of my ancestors,

I give thanks and praise,

for you have given me wisdom and power,

and have now revealed to me what we asked of you.

DANIEL 2:20–23

There is therefore now no condemnation for those who are in Christ Jesus. For the law of the Spirit of life in Christ Jesus has set you free from the law of sin and of death.

ROMANS 8:1–2

Indeed, the word of God is living and active, sharper than any two-edged sword, piercing until it divides soul from spirit, joints from marrow; it is able to judge the thoughts and intentions of the heart.

HEBREWS 4:12

am the gate. Whoever enters by me
will be saved, and will come in and go out
and find pasture. The thief comes only to
steal and kill and destroy. I came that they
may have life, and have it abundantly. I am
the good shepherd. The good shepherd
lays down his life for the sheep.

JOHN 10:9–11

WHOLEHEARTED WORSHIP

I give you thanks, O Lord, with my
　　whole heart....
I bow down toward your holy temple
and give thanks to your name for your
　　steadfast love and your faithfulness;
for you have exalted your name and your word
above everything.
On the day I called, you answered me,
you increased my strength of soul....
Though I walk in the midst of trouble,
you preserve me...;
you stretch out your hand,
and your right hand delivers me.
The Lord will fulfill his purpose for me;
your steadfast love, O Lord, endures forever.
Do not forsake the work of your hands.

PSALM 138:1–3, 7–8

$\mathcal{T}$hen God spoke all these words: I am the Lord your God...; you shall have no other Gods before me. You shall not make for yourself an idol.... You shall not bow down to them or worship them.... You shall not make wrongful use of the name of the Lord your God, for the Lord will not acquit anyone who misuses his name. Remember the sabbath day, and keep it holy. Six days you shall labor and do all your work. But the seventh day is a sabbath to the Lord your God.... Honor your father and your mother, so that your days may be long in the land that the Lord your God is giving you. You shall not murder. You shall not commit adultery. You shall not steal. You shall not bear false witness against your neighbor. You shall not covet...anything that belongs to your neighbor.

EXODUS 20:1–17

So the ransomed of the Lord shall return, and come to Zion with singing; everlasting joy shall be upon their heads; they shall obtain joy and gladness, and sorrow and sighing shall flee away.

ISAIAH 51:11

Rejoice in the Lord always; again I will say, Rejoice. Let your gentleness be known to everyone. The Lord is near. Do not worry about anything, but in everything by prayer and supplication with thanksgiving let your requests be made known to God. And the peace of God, which surpasses all understanding, will guard your hearts and your minds in Christ Jesus.

PHILIPPIANS 4:4–7

UNCONDITIONAL GRATITUDE

*T*hank you, Lord Jesus Christ,
For all the benefits and blessings
Which you have given me,
For all the pains and insults
Which you have borne for me.
Merciful Friend, Brother and Redeemer,
May I know you more clearly,
Love you more dearly,
And follow you more nearly,
Day by day.

RICHARD OF CHICHESTER

$\mathcal{Y}$ou are the light of the world. A city built on a hill cannot be hid. No one after lighting a lamp puts it under the bushel basket, but on the lampstand, and it gives light to all in the house. In the same way, let your light shine before others, so that they may see your good works and give glory to your Father in heaven.

MATTHEW 5:14–16

$\mathcal{N}$ot by might, nor by power, but by my spirit, says the Lord of hosts.

ZECHARIAH 4:6

HEAVEN'S PRAYER

*H*oly, holy, holy,
The Lord God the Almighty,
who was and is and is to come....
You are worthy, our Lord and God,
to receive glory and honor and power,
for you created all things,
and by your will they existed and were created.

REVELATION 4:8, 11

*J*esus said to her, *"I am the resurrection
and the life. Those who believe in me, even
though they die, will live, and everyone who
lives and believes in me will never die. Do
you believe this?"*

JOHN 11:25–26

$\mathcal{T}$herefore, since we are justified by faith, we have peace with God through our Lord Jesus Christ, through whom we have obtained access to this grace in which we stand; and we boast in our hope of sharing the glory of God. And not only that, but we also boast in our sufferings, knowing that suffering produces endurance, and endurance produces character, and character produces hope, and hope does not disappoint us, because God's love has been poured into our hearts through the Holy Spirit that has been given to us. For while we were still weak, at the right time Christ died for the ungodly.

ROMANS 5:1–6

I have said this to you, so that in me you may
have peace. In the world you face persecution.
But take courage; I have conquered the world!

JOHN 16:33

*Humble yourselves therefore under the
mighty hand of God, so that he may exalt
you in due time. Cast all your anxiety on
him, because he cares for you.*

1 PETER 5:6–7

THE BREASTPLATE
OF PATRICK

Christ with me, Christ before me,
    Christ behind me,
Christ in me, Christ beneath me, Christ
    above me,
Christ on my right, Christ on my left,
Christ when I lie down, Christ when I sit
    down, Christ when I arise,
Christ in the heart of every one who thinks
    of me,
Christ in the mouth of every man who
    speaks of me,
Christ in every eye that sees me,
Christ in every ear that hears me.
I arise to-day
Through a mighty strength, the invocation
    of the Trinity,
Through belief in the threeness.
Through confession of the oneness
Of the Creator of Creation.

PATRICK

As God's chosen ones, holy and beloved, clothe yourselves with compassion, kindness, humility, meekness, and patience. Bear with one another and, if anyone has a complaint against another, forgive each other; just as the Lord has forgiven you, so you also must forgive. Above all, clothe yourselves with love, which binds everything together in perfect harmony. And let the peace of Christ rule in your hearts, to which indeed you were called in the one body. And be thankful. Let the word of Christ dwell in you richly; teach and admonish one another in all wisdom; and with gratitude in your hearts sing psalms, hymns, and spiritual songs to God. And whatever you do, in word or deed, do everything in the name of the Lord Jesus, giving thanks to God the Father through him.

COLOSSIANS 3:12–17

*T*hen the king will say to those at his right hand, "Come, you that are blessed by my Father, inherit the kingdom prepared for you from the foundation of the world; for I was hungry and you gave me food, I was thirsty and you gave me something to drink, I was a stranger and you welcomed me, I was naked and you gave me clothing, I was sick and you took care of me, I was in prison and you visited me."…"Truly I tell you, just as you did it to one of the least of these who are members of my family you did it to me."

MATTHEW 25:34–36, 40

THE HEART'S
TRUE HOME

*O*ur hearts are restless, O Lord, until they rest in you.

AUGUSTINE

*V*ery truly, I tell you, unless a grain of wheat falls into the earth and dies, it remains just a single grain; but if it dies, it bears much fruit. Those who love their life lose it, and those who hate their life in this world will keep it for eternal life.

JOHN 12:24–25

*B*ut the Lord said to Samuel, "Do not look on his appearance or on the height of his stature, because I have rejected him; for the Lord does not see as mortals see; they look on the outward appearance, but the Lord looks on the heart."

1 SAMUEL 16:7

*H*e brought me to the banqueting house, and his intention toward me was love.

SONG OF SOLOMON 2:4

Let the same mind be in you that was in
    Christ Jesus,
who, though he was in the form of God,
did not regard equality with God
as something to be exploited,
but emptied himself, taking the form of a slave,
being born in human likeness.
And being found in human form,
he humbled himself
and became obedient to the point of death—
even death on a cross.
Therefore God also highly exalted him and gave
    him the name
that is above every name,
so that at the name of Jesus
every knee should bend,
in heaven and on earth and under the earth,
and every tongue should confess
that Jesus Christ is Lord,
to the glory of God the Father.

PHILIPPIANS 2:5–11

PRAYER FOR UNITY

*M*ay the God of steadfastness and
encouragement grant you to live in harmony
with one another, in accordance with Christ
Jesus, so that together you may with one
voice glorify the God and Father of our
Lord Jesus Christ.

ROMANS 15:5–6

*Since there will never cease to be some in
need on the earth, I therefore command you,
"Open your hand to the poor and needy
neighbor in your land."*

DEUTERONOMY 15:11

*I*f I speak in the tongues of mortals and of angels, but do not have love, I am a noisy gong or a clanging cymbal. And if I have prophetic powers, and understand all mysteries and all knowledge, and if I have all faith, so as to remove mountains, but do not have love, I am nothing. If I give away all my possessions, and if I hand over my body so that I may boast, but do not have love, I gain nothing.

Love is patient; love is kind; love is not envious or boastful or arrogant or rude. It does not insist on its own way; it is not irritable or resentful; it does not rejoice in wrongdoing, but rejoices in the truth. It bears all things, believes all things, hopes all things, endures all things.

Love never ends. But as for prophecies, they will come to an end; as for tongues, they will cease; as for knowledge, it will come to an end. For we know only in part, and we prophesy only in part; but when the complete comes, the partial will come to an end.

When I was a child, I spoke like a child, I thought like a child, I reasoned like a child; when I became an adult, I put an end to childish ways. For now we see in a mirror, dimly, but then we will see face to face. Now I know only in part; then I will know fully, even as I have been fully known. And now faith, hope, and love abide, these three; and the greatest of these is love.

1 CORINTHIANS 13

The Lord, your God, is in your midst, a warrior who gives victory; he will rejoice over you with gladness, he will renew you in his love; he will exult over you with loud singing.

ZEPHANIAH 3:17

DISCERNMENT

*G*od, give us grace to accept with
serenity the things that cannot be changed,
courage to change the things that should
be changed, and wisdom to distinguish the
one from the other.

REINHOLD NIEBUHR

*J*esus said to him, "I am the way, and
the truth, and the life. No one comes to the
Father except through me."

JOHN 14:6

*L*et mutual love continue. Do not neglect to show hospitality to strangers, for by doing that some have entertained angels without knowing it.

HEBREWS 13:1–2

*L*et justice roll down like waters, and righteousness like an ever-flowing stream.

AMOS 5:24

The Lord is my shepherd, I shall not want.
He makes me lie down in green pastures;
he leads me beside still waters;
he restores my soul. He leads me in right paths
for his name's sake.
Even though I walk through the darkest valley,
I fear no evil; for you are with me;
your rod and your staff—
they comfort me.
You prepare a table before me
in the presence of my enemies;
you anoint my head with oil;
my cup overflows.
Surely goodness and mercy shall follow me
all the days of my life,
and I shall dwell in the house of the Lord
my whole life long.

PSALM 23

APPENDIX 1—BIBLE PRAYERS

APPENDIX 2—FAMOUS PRAYERS

APPENDIX 3